CONTEMPORARY
PRAYERS

to
whatever
works

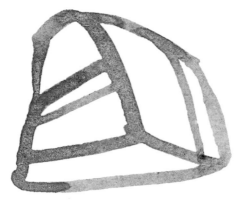

An Artist's Collection of
Prayers to Nothing-in-Particular

CONTEMPORARY
PRAYERS
to
whatever
works

HANNAH BURR

TILLER PRESS

New York   London   Toronto   Sydney   New Delhi

TILLER PRESS

An Imprint of Simon & Schuster, Inc.
1230 Avenue of the Americas
New York, NY 10020

First Tiller Press trade paperback edition March 2021

TILLER PRESS and colophon are trademarks of Simon & Schuster, Inc.

For information about special discounts for bulk purchases, please contact Simon & Schuster Special Sales at 1-866-506-1949 or business@simonandschuster.com.

The Simon & Schuster Speakers Bureau can bring authors to your live event. For more information or to book an event, contact the Simon & Schuster Speakers Bureau at 1-866-248-3049 or visit our website at www.simonspeakers.com.

Interior design by Jennifer Chung

Manufactured in China

10 9 8 7 6 5 4 3 2 1

Library of Congress Cataloging-in-Publication Data
Names: Burr, Hannah, 1973- author.
Title: Contemporary prayers to whatever works : an artist's collection of prayers to nothing-in-particular / Hannah Burr. | Description: New York : Tiller Press, 2021. | Includes bibliographical references. | Identifiers: LCCN 2020021257 (print) | LCCN 2020021258 (ebook) | ISBN 9781982154677 (paperback) | ISBN 9781982154684 (ebook) | Subjects: LCSH: Prayers.
Classification: LCC BL560 .B824 2021 (print) | LCC BL560 (ebook) | DDC 204/.33—dc23

LC record available at https://lccn.loc.gov/2020021257
LC ebook record available at https://lccn.loc.gov/2020021258

ISBN 978-1-9821-5467-7
ISBN 978-1-9821-5468-4 (ebook)

To

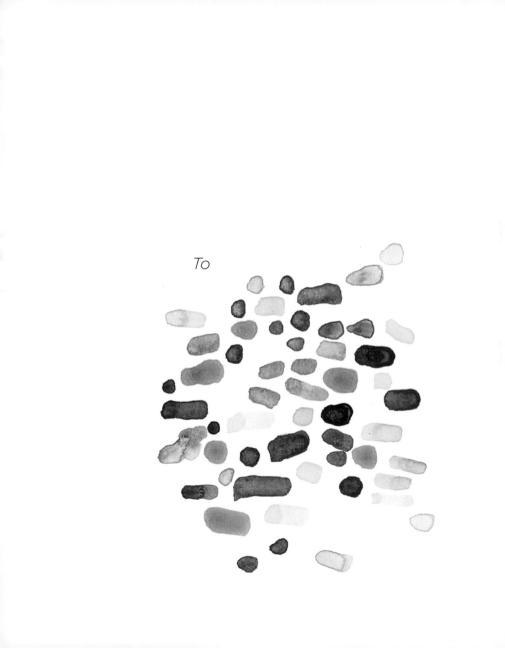

CONTENTS

INTRODUCTION

This book is an artist's take on prayers, written in plain language to whomever or whatever works for you. It's one in a series intended for anybody, regardless of belief. It sidesteps the whole debate about what one personally feels connected to, and instead focuses on the act of connection itself.

The images in this book aren't supposed to resemble anything in particular. They have been paired at random with the phrases, and painted with acrylic gouache pigment on paper. They are abstract forms that can stand in for whatever you might want to address in a prayer or petition. What you address is your business: it could be a mythic warrior princess or a plastic bottle, Jesus or Great Spirit, or a force like gravity, art, or the ocean. Some prayers include other dash- or dot-like images, which you can fill in with whatever person, place, thing, or scenario is currently in heavy rotation in your thoughts and feelings.

Sections like "Yes" offer prompts for noting the action of prayer, expressions of gratitude, and a little creative brainstorming. These are a means of redirecting thought when it tends to slide into shadow territory, particularly when the shadows begin to engulf and overwhelm. Play around with them and see how and when they work for you.

You don't have to understand or have a clear idea of what you believe in to pray; it can be fuzzy, and your experience may change over time. I find that the more I engage in prayer of this kind, the less I understand what I'm praying to and yet the more intimate the relationship becomes.

You also don't need anybody's permission or intercession to connect directly with ◈. No one is more qualified than you, though others may be more familiar with the practice.

Lastly, this is a come-as-you-are affair. There's no need to be eloquent or pious to engage in prayer. I find it's best not to BS, sugarcoat, or be overly formal in my prayers. Honesty is the very medium of this whole process. Phrases like the ones in this book help me to touch ground and admit my smallness, and by so doing connect to a broader freedom and peace, similar to what I experience beside an expanse of ocean or looking up at a big sky.

I'm writing this introduction in April 2020, when the world is collectively experiencing alarming and sudden upheaval, over which we seem to have little to no control. We are a species in free fall with an uncertain future. This may have always been true, but it is nearly impossible to ignore at this moment in history. These phrases were mostly written in response to personal circumstances at an earlier time, and yet strike me as highly relevant and practical for right now, too. May they assist you and those you love in navigating whatever is in front of you at present and surround you with ⬭ in the details of your day.

ON SLOW

Quiet my mind,  ,

and show me what's next.

Help me,  ,

to think like a piece of wood,
or a plant.

Just for a little while.

Can you help me,
get off the couch?
Or, if I'm supposed to be resting here,
help me to let myself be,
and give myself a pass for now.

I'm tired and depleted.

, help me to rest.

Help me,  ,

to take in the specific arrangement
of objects in front of me,

to really see the details.

 , show me how to listen to,

care for, and rest
in this only body I have.

 , even in this completely
unrecognizable situation,

I'm feeling okay and trusting in you.

If you'd prefer I be wigging out,
please let me know.

FAST BRAIN

There's a code-red emergency going on
in this human brain of mine!

Please,  ,

help me to drop down into the
grounding shelter of the body.

I'm overwhelmed,  .

 , I can't seem to

stay away from .

Please help!

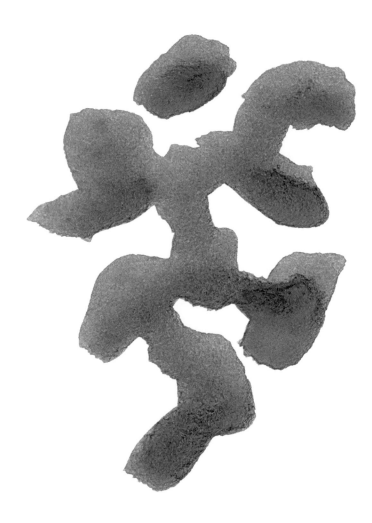

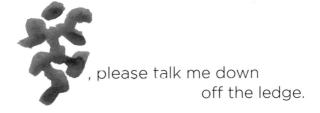, please talk me down
                    off the ledge.

 , I need your help.

I'm in obsession and the brain won't stop!

Please direct my attention to
                    where you want it.

NOPE

What. The. F.

Not. Okay.

This is my prayer,  .

Everything feels ashen and gray.

Can you help me,  ,

to reconnect with joy
and delight?

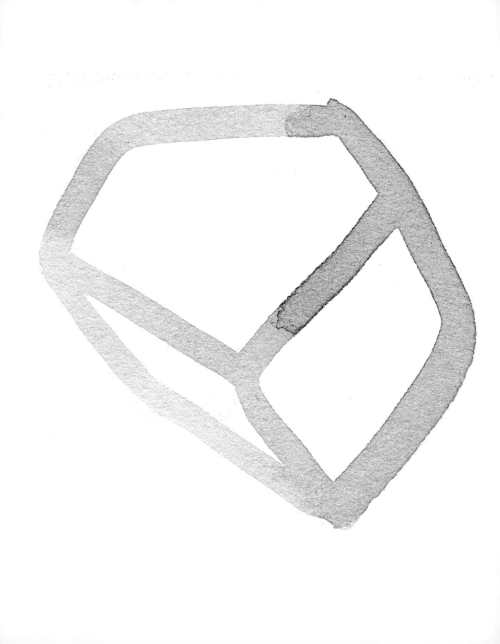

I gotta be honest, 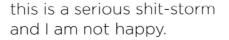,

this is a serious shit-storm
and I am not happy.

This is my honest and
only offering right now.

What an uncomfortable situation!

I can't seem to either swallow this
                              or spit it out.

See me through this,

please,    .

, I am in RESISTANCE.

Like a donkey pulling backward in full bray,
I am NOT going along smilingly here.

It's a real throw-down.

That was not okay,  .

I keep replaying it.

Help me to let this move through me
without making things worse.

My hackles are seriously UP.

Please,  ,

surround and protect me
    from my own disturbed thinking.

STAY HERE

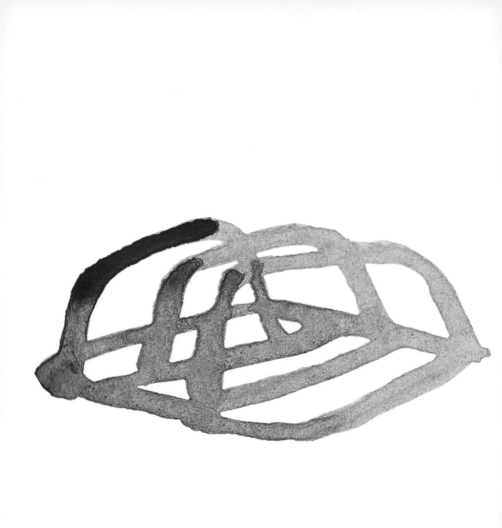

Help me,  ,

to be present for  ,

fully here and in my body.

Help me notice the details, 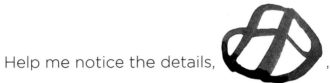,

the ones that matter,
the subtle sparkly underlayer to things.

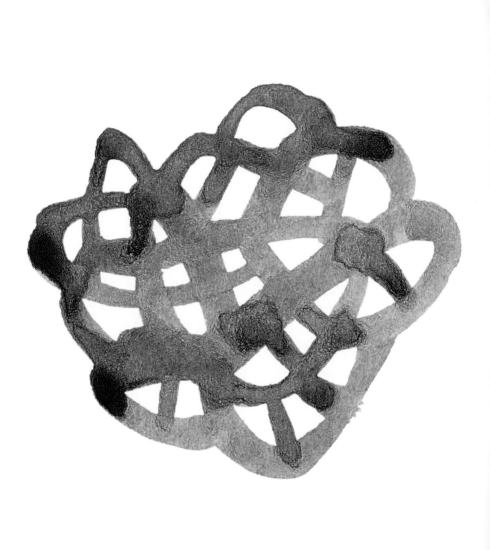

Thank you,  ,

for being the tree in my yard
and the chair that I'm sitting in.*

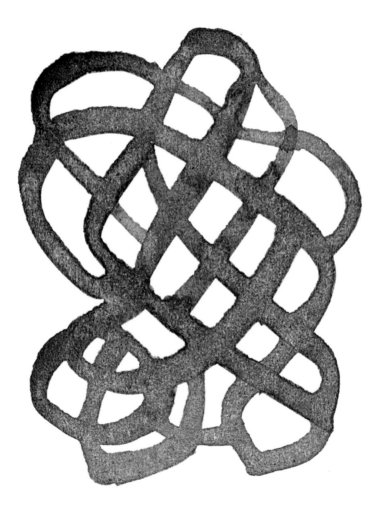

Help me,  ,

to find you via the senses,
right here and now.

Here's what I see:

Here's what I smell:

Here's what I hear:

, help me drop the idea
of past and future

for the what and who that is here,
right in front of me, just now.

Thank you,  ,

for being the very situation.

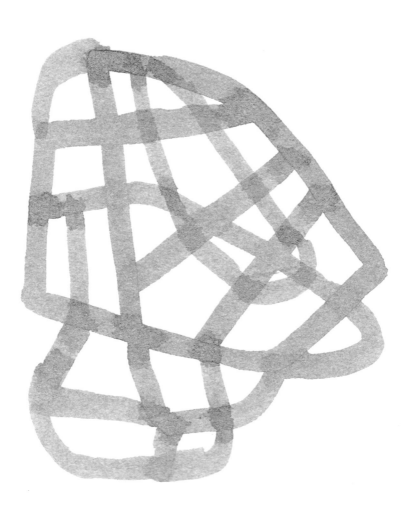

, here is where I felt your
presence and love

in the day:

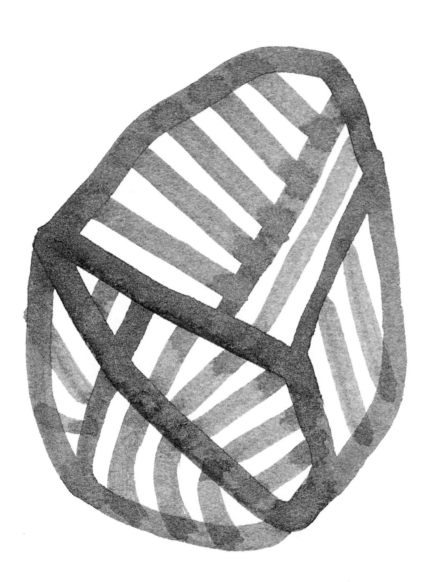

Help me,  ,

to reconnect with
what matters and what lasts.

Help me not to try to figure out
what these are.

DREAD

Okay,  ,

I'm officially spooked!

Help bring me back down
into the body and legs.

Thank you.

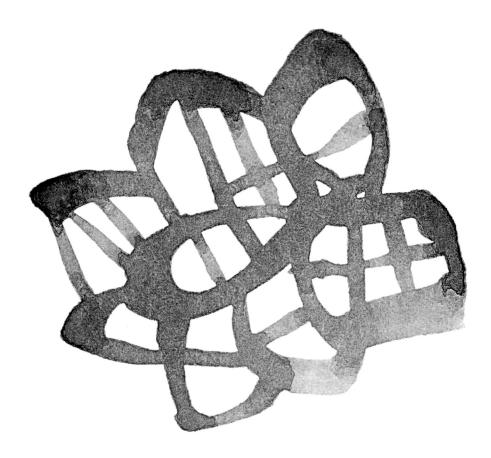

My whole system feels wrecked:
shaky, jittery, and off-balance.

Please,  ,

smooth out this whole vibe going on.

Thanks.

Remind me,  ,

    that this, like everything,
        won't last forever.

That I've been in a similar place before
and it worked out okay.

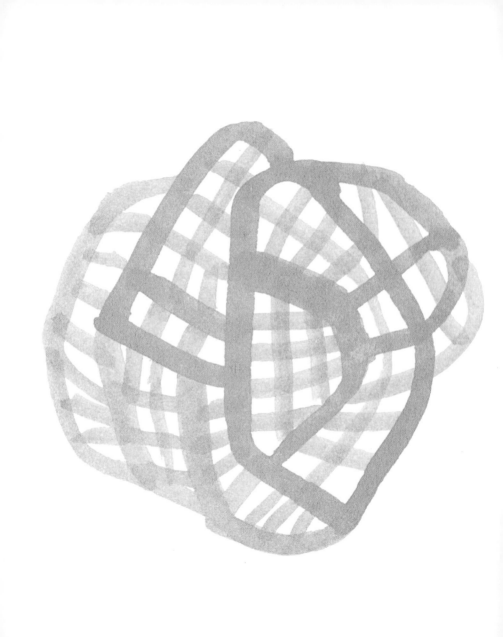

In my thinking and stories, ,

this is a disaster.

Can you help me see otherwise?

Show me, ,

the difference between humiliation

and humility.

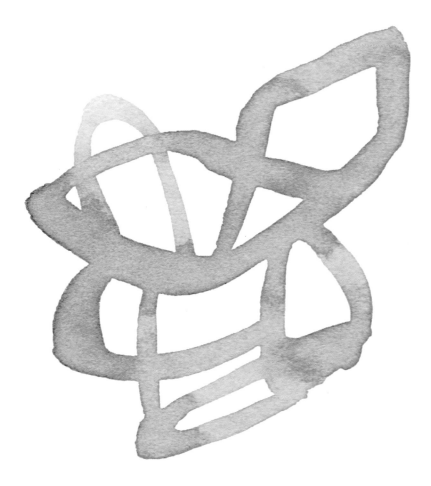

I've lost my sense of humor,  .

I'd love to find myself laughing
        at something at silent-laugh
            or snort-level today.

Thank you.

I leave with you,  ,

the following
  disquieting concerns: .

And I thank you for

      and   .

OTHERS

Help me, , to let others be.

Help me, , to let myself be.

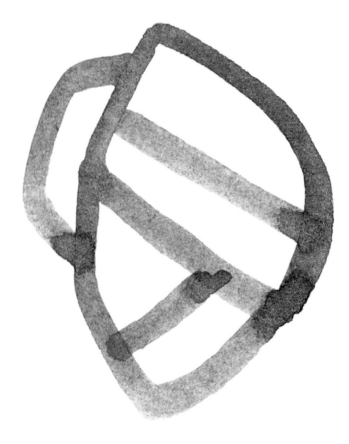

Please guide and
inspire this 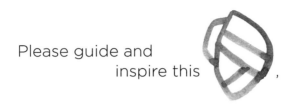 ,

and everyone involved.

Help it flow.

Make it astonishingly easy,
and also delightful for all of us.

I keep wanting to
change, fix,
or influence  .

Please,  ,

help me stay in my
own Hula-Hoop here.

Show me how to be
supportive here, ,

and how to "shut it"
when I might otherwise cause harm.

Help me to enjoy my life, ,

the people I meet,
the things I do.

 , help me to drop the
hero complex

and show me how to
serve without fanfare.

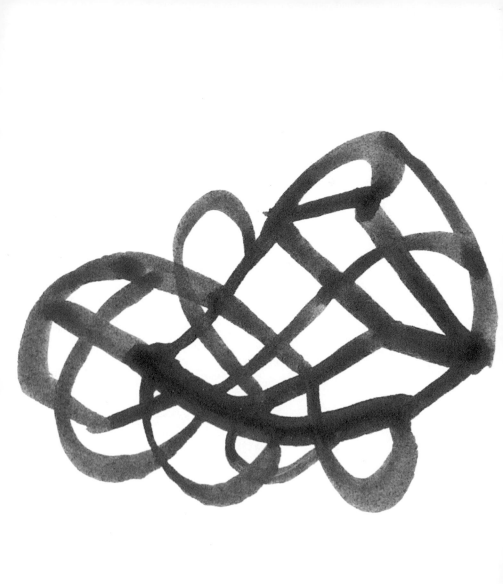

Help me, ,

to be free of attachment or aversion,

while still continuing to care.*

OFFERING

Help me,  ,

to let all of this be,

even the squelchy parts.

I know  isn't working

but I'm not yet willing to let it go.

Help me, , to be willing.

, I really don't want to,

but I offer up to you.

I leave in your care

and trust this will work out okay,
even if I can't imagine how right now.

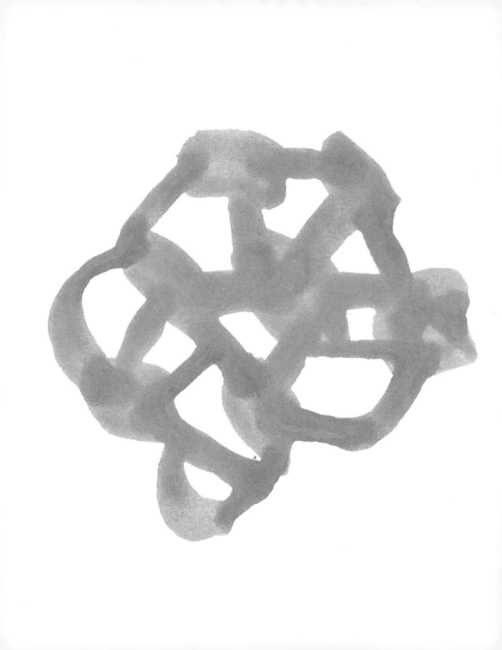

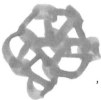 , help me to pry open this death grip

I have on .

Please redirect my focus.

, help me stand in the truth

and let go of the outcome.

Here,  ,

is what I place on the makeshift

altar/drop-off-the-cliff edge:

Please,  ,

be the doer of this day.*

INNER KID

How,   , may I treat myself

like I might treat a baby otter,
a baby cheetah,
or a wobbly spring lamb?

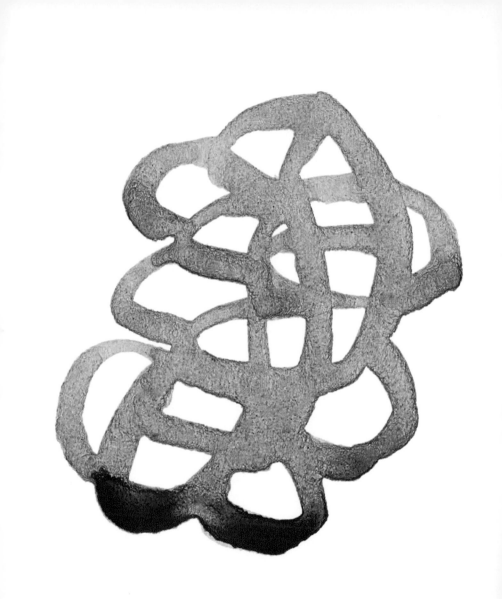

Help me,  ,

to see everyone around me,
and myself,

like toddlers bumbling around
playing dress-up.

I'd love to feel wonder
and awe,  ,

like a kid—
please make it so!

Help me, ,

to slip out of this jaded,
cynical, and blamey attitude

and into something that feels more
right-sized and comfortable.

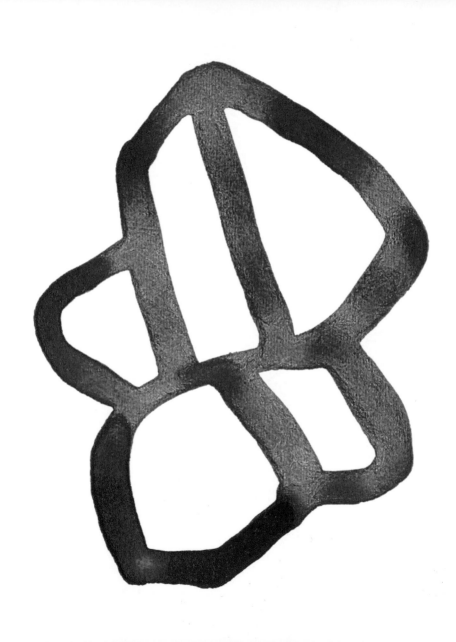

Show me,  ,

how to say YES

even to the messy,

the ugly, and the awkward

in myself and in others.

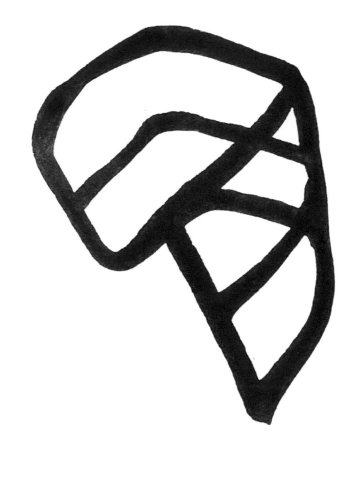

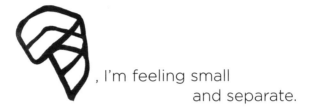, I'm feeling small
and separate.

Please plug me back in.

May I trust you,  ,

and take you with me all places.*

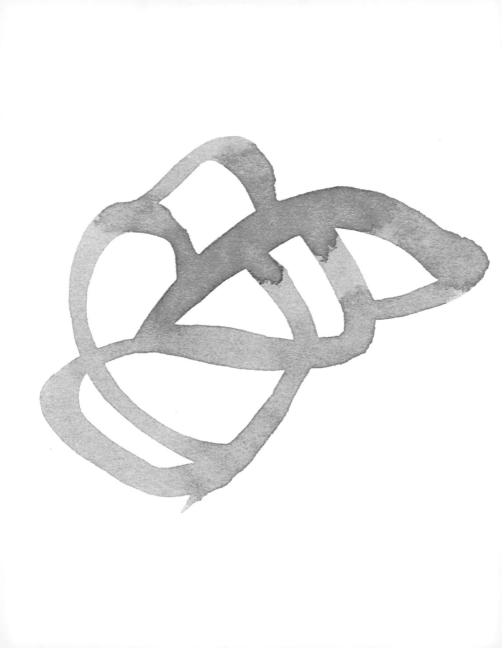

, you are in charge and,

weirdly somehow,
beyond my understanding.

Please show me how to be in flow
and connected to you
throughout this day.

 , will you help me

fall in love with my own life,
my own body,

my own self?

WAY THROUGH

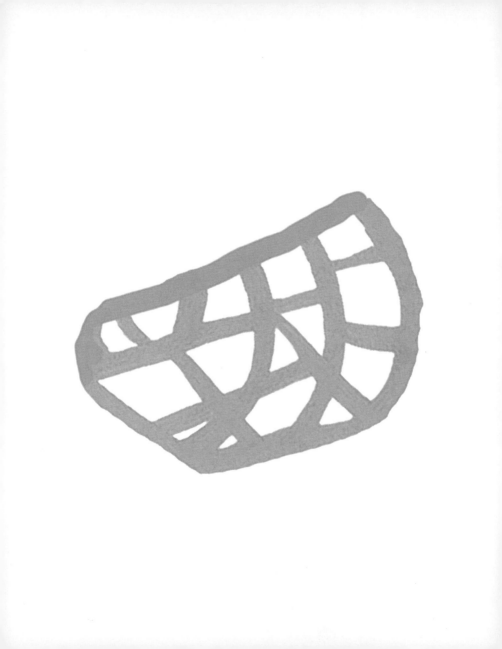

I'm at a crossroads  .

Which way should I go?

There's got to be a better way,  .

Will you show me?

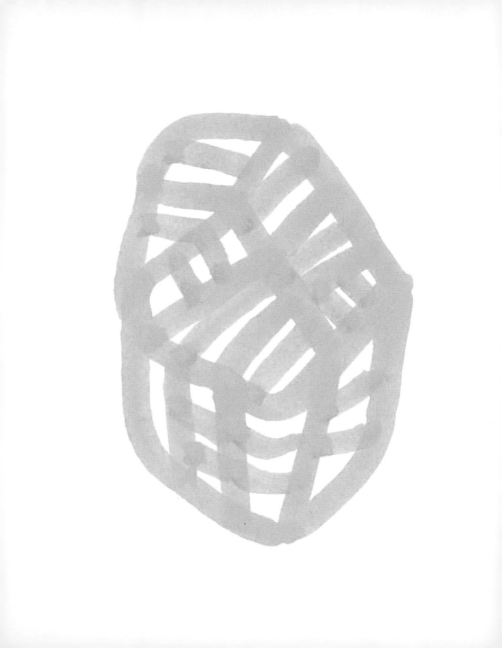

, I've never been here before.

Are you still here with me?

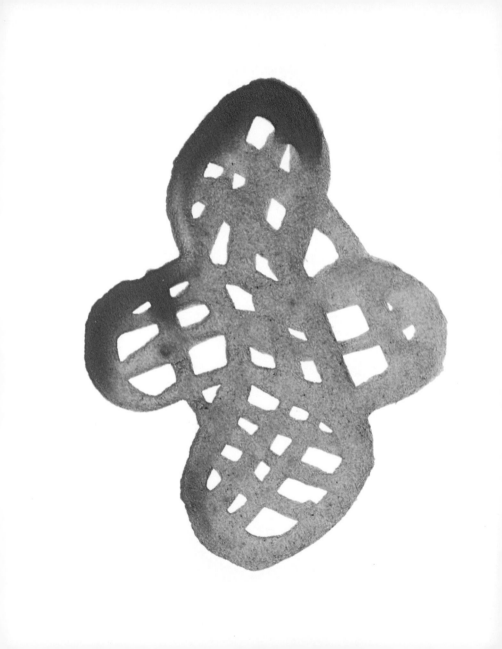

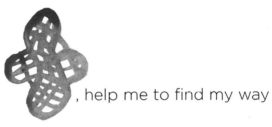, help me to find my way

through the unfamiliar light
of this situation/day.

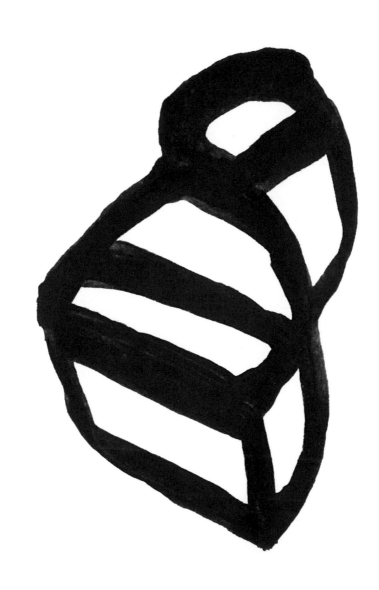

Up is down
and down is up!

Where are you, , in all of this?

I'd like to feel your presence
palpably with me,
in and all around me.

, it feels like things have changed
and they might not ever
be the same.

I want you as my through line.

Please be with me from now on.

Despite all the tantalizing distractions,

I will look for you,  ,

in this day.

Please,  ,

go before me into this interaction
    so that you're there before I get there;

may I trust in your presence
    in every detail of the
        unfolding situation.

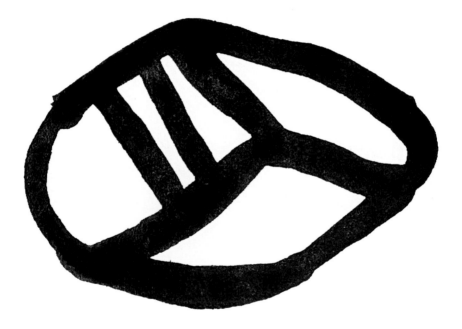

Wow.

This is heavy.

Help me stay with this.

Help me move through.

NEW VIEW

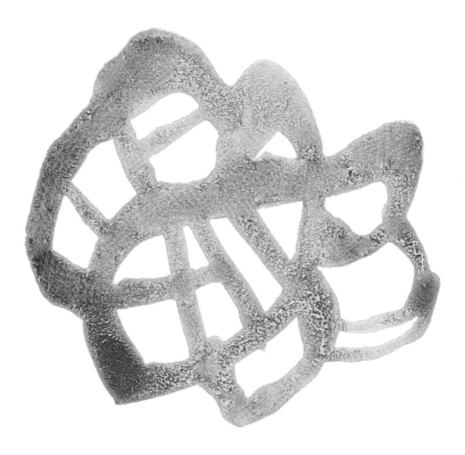

 , how might this be
the best thing

that could be happening to me?

Help me to see this with fresh eyes.

Illuminate my view,  ,

surprise and inspire me—please!

Help me,  ,

to sit back and
let all of these events unfold

with their strange and uncanny precision,
as they do,

no meddling needed from me.

, I'm taking this super personally.

Can you bring a new perspective wherein
I'm not the center of all orbits?

Help me,  ,

to see beauty in details today,
even in trash blowing by.

Let me see its singularity and perfection.

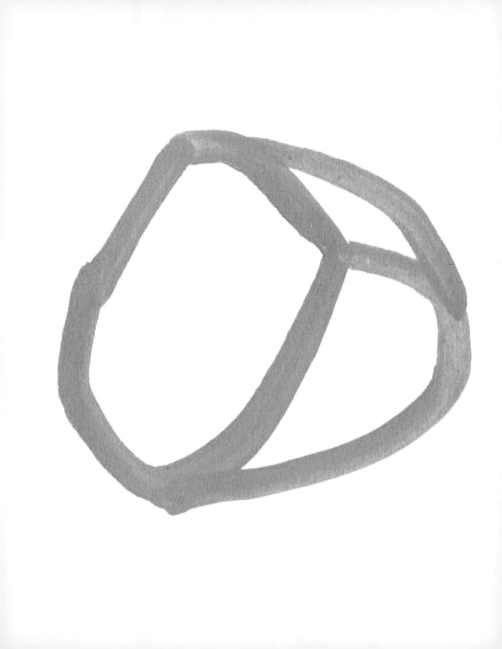

Help me to be truly honest
          with myself,  .

Help me to look at things without
     distortion, blinders, or special filters.

Where things seem solid
        and fixed in place,  ,

   help me to see the possibility of
            motion and change.

Where I see a small part up close,
        help me to also see a vast expanding.

Inspire me, ,

toward what you want for me.

Help me to lose interest in what doesn't
ultimately serve your purposes.

YES

Help me,  ,

to want what I have.

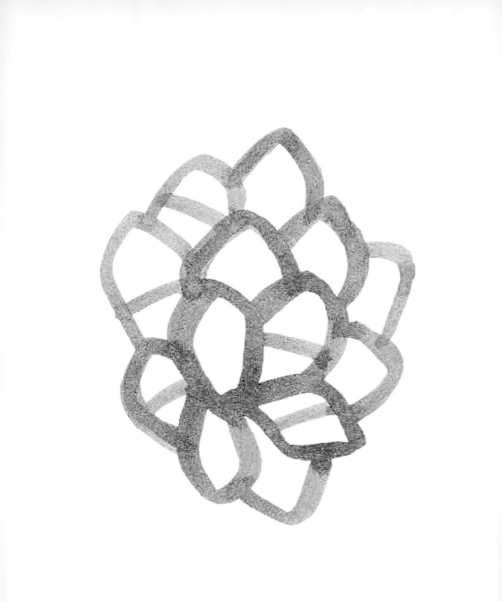

Help me, ,

to enjoy the ride:

the twists and turns,
bumps and all.

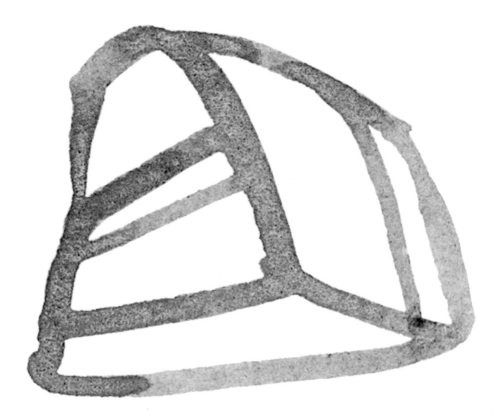

Thank you,  ,

for the dreamlike adventure of this life.

Help me to be curious, to get into it
instead of shying away from it.

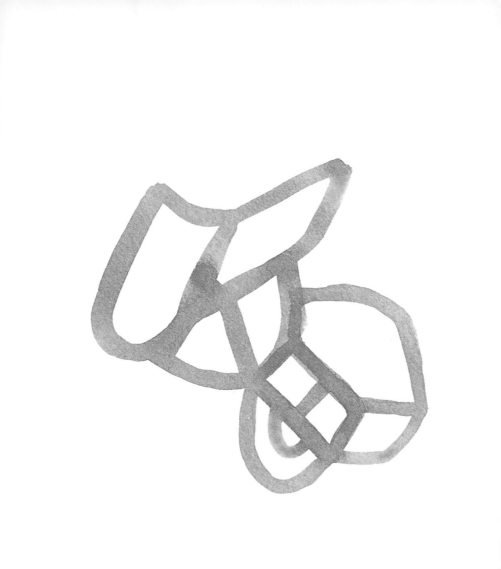

 , here's what I loved

about today:

These, ,

are my absolute favorite things

in the world:

Thank you!

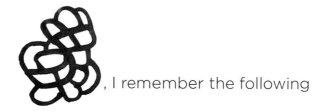 , I remember the following

joy-filled moments:

More like this, please!

, here's what I want to

acknowledge and

appreciate about today:

, and ,

and ,

and also .

Thank you,  ,

for this particular weather pattern

and its interesting qualities of ,

 , and .

I'm grateful right now,  ,

for  .

Today,
I would love to experience ,

 , and .

ACKNOWLEDGMENTS

Thank you Thank you Thank you Thank you Thank you Thank you Thank you Thank you Thank you Thank you Thank you Thank you

Ron Denhardt, Paula Breen, Josephine Burr, Stephanie Chace, Jennifer Chung, Kate Davids, Anne Emerson, Theresa DiMasi, Laura Flavin, Allison Har-zvi, Benjamin Holmes, Lauren Hummel, Andrew Innes, Samantha Lubash, Guy Marshall, Sue Murad, Lauren Ollerhead, Marge O'Neil, Rosanne Rooney, Patrick Sullivan, Jessica Tenbusch

NOTES

51   This prayer was originally printed in *Contemporary Prayers to * [whatever works]* by Hannah Burr in 2013.

93   Adapted from the *Visuddhimagga Buddhaghosa*, a treatise on Buddhism written in the fifth century CE by Buddhaghosa and referenced often in contemporary Buddhist writing.

109   This prayer was originally printed in *Help me [   ], do the thing* by Hannah Burr in 2016.

125   This phrasing is inspired by the poem "love is a place" by e. e. cummings.

INDEX